THE H. P. LOVECRAFT
DRAWING BOOK

THE H. P. LOVECRAFT
DRAWING BOOK

LEARN TO DRAW STRANGE SCENES OF OTHERWORLDLY HORROR

ARCTURUS

ARCTURUS

This edition published in 2018 by Arcturus Publishing Limited
26/27 Bickels Yard, 151–153 Bermondsey Street,
London SE1 3HA

ISBN: 978-1-78888-215-6
AD006389US

Printed in China

CONTENTS

Introduction

Portrait of Lovecraft.

"*It represented a monster of vaguely anthropoid outline, but with an octopus-like head whose face was a mass of feelers, a scaly, rubbery-looking body, prodigious claws on hind and fore feet, and long, narrow wings behind.*"

So begins a description of undoubtedly Howard Phillips Lovecraft's most famous creation—Cthulhu, High Priest of "The Great Old Ones" in "The Call of Cthulhu," first published in the American magazine, *Weird Tales,* in 1928.

Born in 1890 in Providence, Rhode Island, Lovecraft's prolific writings were mainly published during his life in so-called "pulp" magazines such as *Weird Tales*—stories such as "At the Mountains of Madness," "The Other Gods," and "The Rats in the Walls." Although Lovecraft never succeeded in making much of a living from his writing, the influence of his stories has continued to resonate down the years, inspiring many modern writers, such as Stephen King and Neil Gaiman.

Before his death in 1937 at the age of 46, Lovecraft had given the world a universe of weird supernatural beings, elder gods, creeping horrors, and mind-bending realities. His ideas were expanded upon both by writers contemporary to him, such as Robert Bloch and Robert E. Howard, and those subsequent to his death, such as August Derleth, the writer who coined the term "The Cthulhu Mythos" for this shared universe.

The Cthulhu Mythos has inspired creators to this day, resulting in adaptations to comic strips, films, music, and games, particularly the role-playing game *Call of Cthulhu* and video games such as *Call of Cthulhu: Dark Corners of the Earth.*

Countless artists have attempted to depict Lovecraft's creations, a task not always made easy by the often deliberately vague descriptions employed within his stories, such as: "They were amorphous lumps of viscous black slime that took temporary shapes for various purposes"—"The Mound," first published in *Weird Tales,* 1940.

Cthulhu is one of the creatures for whom a detailed description is provided, with Lovecraft even producing a sketch of it himself.

But where can we look for visual inspiration to interpret his other creations for ourselves?

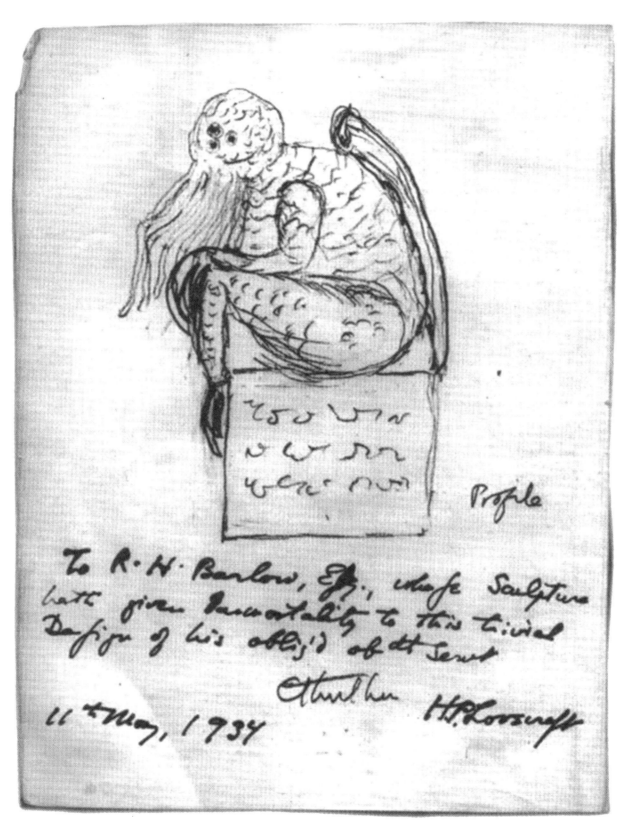

A sketch of a Cthulhu, drawn by H. P. Lovecraft in 1934.

Useful visual influences

Lovecraft's descriptions often reference an amalgam of existing living creatures, humanoid forms, and extinct animals: "There flopped rhythmically a horde of tame, trained, hybrid winged things. They were not altogether crows, nor moles, nor buzzards, nor ants, nor vampire bats, nor decomposed human beings; They flopped limply along, half with their webbed feet and half with their membranous wings."—The Byakhee, described in "The Festival," first published in *Weird Tales*, 1925.

Sea life, in particular, seems to have been a great source of inspiration for Lovecraft. Cthulhu is described as having a cephalopod head:

octopuses, squid, cuttlefish, and nautilidae all provide good visual material. Tentacles, in particular, have come to be associated with Lovecraftian fiction and the leaps in undersea filming technology for programs such as the BBC's *The Blue Planet* provide us with ever weirder and more alien-looking creatures from the depths.

Other sea life such as fish, sea slugs and cucumbers, crustaceans such as crabs and lobsters, sea anemones, and jellyfish can look like something straight out of Lovecraft's stories—just imagine an Atolla jellyfish floating nebulously in the air in front of you, rather than in the sea, add in a human-looking eye in the center, and you have the makings of something truly horrific.

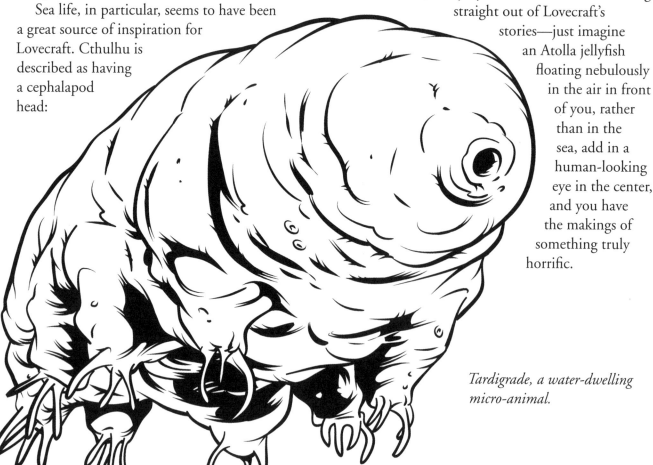

Tardigrade, a water-dwelling micro-animal.

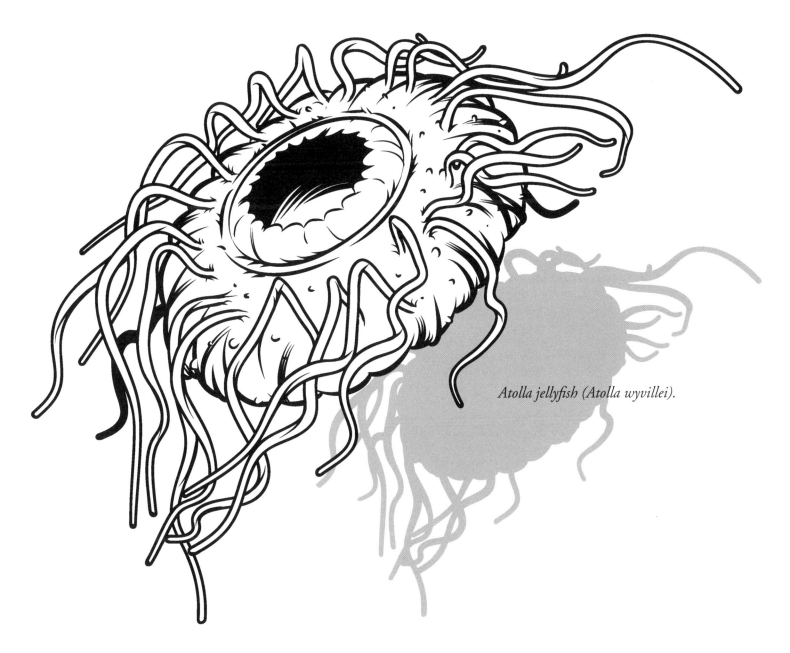

Atolla jellyfish (Atolla wyvillei).

Microscopic and miniature worlds can also be mined for inspiration—bizarre-looking amoebae and viruses along with insect and arachnid forms such as tics, fleas, centipedes, caterpillars, etc. Check out pictures of the microscopic water-dwelling tardigrade and you may never sleep again!

Certain textures crop up again and again in Lovecraft's descriptions—slime, ooze, scales, leathery or membranous skin, etc. Seek out creatures with these qualities, such as bats,

crocodilians, amphibians, etc. and combine them with sea life, insects and arachnid forms or with other animal, human, and anthropoid forms. And don't forget about prehistoric life to provide inspiration for spines, claws, teeth, etc.

Spawn, egg sacs, cocoons, flora, and fungi, such as the Veiled Lady or Devil's Fingers can also provide interesting forms to play around with.

Look around you—there's a world of influence to draw from!

Inspiration from art

"Daily life had for him come to be a phantasmagoria of macabre shadow-studies; now glittering and leering with concealed rottenness as in Beardsley's best manner, now hinting terrors behind the commonest shapes and objects as in the subtler and less obvious work of Gustave Doré."

—"The Horror at Red Hook," first published in *Weird Tales* in 1927.

Lovecraft's world of half-glimpsed, sanity-twisting revelations lurking in the shadows or at the corner of perception lends itself well to other interpretations of the macabre and surreal in art. In addition to Aubrey Beardsley and Gustave Doré (Dante's *Inferno*), interpreters of the surreal and macabre include 15th century Dutch painter Hieronymus Bosch, whose nightmarish visions included paintings such as *The Garden of Earthly Delights* and *The Temptation of St. Anthony* and, more recently, the surrealist work of artists such as Salvador Dalí and photographic manipulator William Mortensen.

If you want to look beyond Lovecraft's menagerie of creatures, you will also find descriptions of geometry that defy the senses and architecture that should not exist, such as "the nightmare corpse-city of R'lyeh... loathsomely redolent of spheres and dimensions apart from ours" ("The Call of Cthulhu," 1928). German expressionist cinema such as *The Cabinet of Dr. Caligari* (1920) utilizes warped geometry to depict its sets in a way that unsettles the eye. Dutch graphic artist M. C. Escher also utilized optical illusions to create objects and landscapes that defy the senses, such as in his wood engraving *Other World* (1947) or his lithograph *Relativity* (1953).

More recent inspiration can be found in the work of artists of the macabre, such as Swiss painter and designer H. R. Giger. Two early collections of Giger's work, titled *Necronomicon I and II,* were named after the fictional grimoire created by Lovecraft for his 1924 story "The Hound." Giger's design for the creature in the film *Alien* has become an iconic image and was based on his painting *Necronom IV.*

American fantasy artist Brom is a frequent contributor of macabre and fantastical art to role-playing and card games such as *Magic: The Gathering.* He creates commercial but often disturbing imagery, drawing on emaciation, body modification, and mutation.

Contemporaries working with similarly dark imagery include Russian artist Stray Child and American artist Erik M. Gist.

Comic artists such as Mike Mignola (*Hellboy*, Dark Horse Comics), James Harren (*B. P. R. D.*, Dark Horse Comics; *Rumble*, Image Comics) and Guy Davis (*B. P. R. D.*, *The Marquis*, Dark Horse Comics) also create some inspiringly dark imagery and grotesquery. Davis has subsequently worked as a concept artist on films such as Guillermo del Toro's *The Shape of Water.* It is worth checking out these artist's sketchbook sections in graphic novels for an insight into the creative process behind their creations. Instagram feeds and personal blogs can also provide a source of sketchbook and development art, as well as more finished pieces.

With the rise in popularity of video games and the increasing sophistication of special-effects work in film and TV, it is also worth looking at the work of concept artists, such as the aforementioned Guy Davis, or Keith Thompson, another frequent collaborator with filmmaker Guillermo del Toro (*Pan's Labyrinth*). There is a wealth of concept art available online or it is often collected into book form for specific video games and films, and again can provide great insight into the creative process.

So—you have a blank piece of paper or a computer screen sitting in front of you. Where do you start creating your other worlds?

The Temptation of St Anthony *by Hieronymus Bosch.*

Basic techniques

Pencilling

The traditional pencil is still one of the oldest and most versatile ways of producing a variety of lines and tones. They come in a selection of hardnesses, ranging from something that will barely make a mark on your paper to leads that are so soft they will allow you to produce a dense black mark or soft, blendable tone. It is good to have a range of hardnesses available according to the task at hand, as we shall see.

An alternative is a "mechanical" pencil, which holds an extendable lead of fixed thickness. Mechanical pencils are available in a number of widths and leads and are usually also available in a variety of hardnesses, although generally not as wide a range as that of traditional pencils. The advantage of a mechanical pencil is that it doesn't need constant sharpening in the way that a traditional pencil does, but it also can't be angled in the same way that a traditional pencil can, to change the quality of the line. Depending on the thickness and hardness of your lead, mechanical pencils can also be prone to breakage. It's worth investing in good-quality leads from an art shop. Something like a 0.5 mm B lead should be strong enough to avoid too much breakage, but for greater strength move up to a 0.7 mm lead if you can.

One problem when drawing can be ending up with a morass of dense lines, so much so that you lose sight of what you are trying to draw. There are a few ways to minimize this:

Start off lightly with a hard pencil, 2H or even 4H, which will give you a very faint line but which will be sufficient to sketch out outlines and main shapes. As you add more detail to your drawing, increase the amount of pressure you use and start to use a softer leaded pencil. 2B is a good hardness to achieve a reasonably dark final line.

Another possibility is starting off drawing with a colored lead (traditionally blue), with which you can construct your drawing before finishing off in black. This allows the final pencil to be added without getting mixed up with the lines you've already produced. Don't use this method if your pencil drawing is to be the final product, however, as you will be left with the blue line underneath your drawing. This technique was originally developed for artwork to be scanned in for printing, at which point the blue would be photographically filtered out, leaving just the black line (it's a technique that some comic-strip artists still use). If you're scanning your drawing into something like Photoshop for working on digitally, it is relatively easy to filter out the blue lines.

Don't feel confined to just one piece of paper either—a light box (a flat lighted sheet over which you place your paper) can be used to retrace your drawing, as long as the paper you're using isn't too heavy. It's also useful to be able to flip your drawing over to check how it looks the other way round—a sure way to show up any mistakes in what you're drawing. Budget light boxes (such as LED ones) are readily available, or you can make your own by positioning a lamp (with a cool bulb, such as an energy-efficient one) underneath an angled sheet

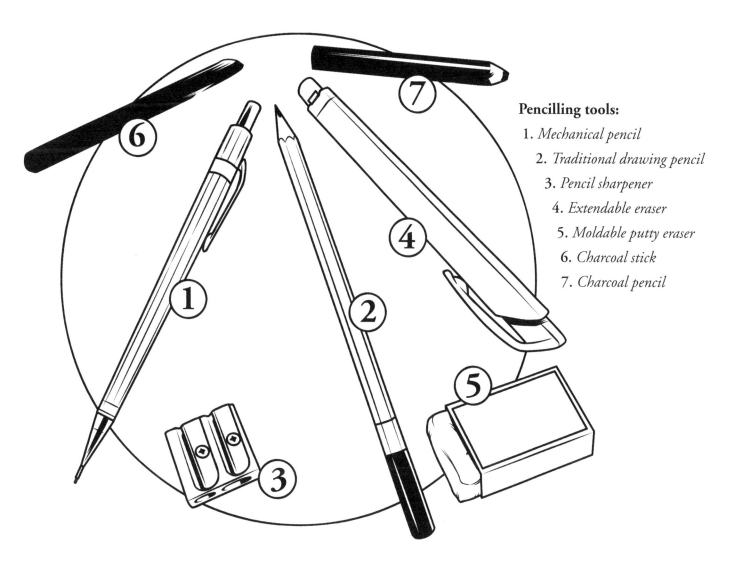

Pencilling tools:

1. *Mechanical pencil*
2. *Traditional drawing pencil*
3. *Pencil sharpener*
4. *Extendable eraser*
5. *Moldable putty eraser*
6. *Charcoal stick*
7. *Charcoal pencil*

of Perspex (don't use glass, as you will be putting pressure on it and it could shatter).

Blended tone is best added with a softer pencil, pastel, or charcoal. These can all be messy, however, and it's best if you spray a "fixative" over them after you have finished to prevent smudging (hairspray is a cheap alternative to artist's fixative, although you will end up with a perfumed drawing).

Other equipment to consider buying includes a battery-powered or electric pencil sharpener

(a sharp pencil is much easier to use to achieve good linework), an extendable eraser (for erasing smaller areas), and a moldable "putty" eraser.

If you are going to work on your drawing digitally, pencil drawings can be scanned directly into a computer and "cleaned up" in a program such as Photoshop by adjusting contrast settings and levels etc. and by digitally erasing unwanted areas. The other alternative is to finish your drawing off in ink…

Inking

Inking is essentially going over your pencil drawing with an ink-based medium. If you want to preserve your pencil drawing, you can always do this on a separate piece of paper using tracing paper or a light box. There are now also a variety of digital inking methods that you can use—more on which later.

If you are going to be using a wet medium with your line drawing (ink wash or watercolor, for example), it is vital that you use a waterproof medium with which to ink—a dip pen or brush with India ink, for instance, or a waterproof fiber-tip or marker pen. Many fiber-tip and fountain pen inks will just dissolve when wet, so do a test piece beforehand if that's what you intend to do. If your final piece is purely linework, or is to be scanned into a computer, you can really use any medium you like that will make a black mark. These include:

Dip pen and ink—a metal nib inserted into a holder and dipped into liquid ink. Drawing nibs are available in various widths and flexibilities—the more flexible the nib, the wider the variation achievable in the line, according to the amount of pressure used. Dip pens can be scratchy, however, and prone to catching on rougher papers, resulting in unwanted ink spatter. Ink can also take a long time to dry, so be aware of possible smudging.

Brush and ink—one of the most versatile inking methods, but one that takes a good deal of practice. With practice, however, it is possible to achieve a smooth, flowing line—much less scratchy than that of a dip pen. Brushes are available in a wide variety of sizes and styles. A good watercolor brush with a fine point is probably best to begin with. Angle and pressure can be varied to produce a range of styles. You can also use a "dry brush" technique by wiping most of the ink off your brush before you apply it to create a rougher, more textured look. Again, a smoother paper will give you a smoother line, but a rougher watercolor paper can give more textured results. If you're using waterproof ink, be sure to wash out your brush thoroughly before it dries. Many a good brush has been lost due to neglect!

Fiber-tip and marker pens—whilst these pens don't generally have the flexibility of the previous two methods, they are very convenient to use and variations in line thickness can be achieved by going over the same line several times. Larger marker pens can be useful for filling in large areas of black. They are also very useful for carrying around with you for drawing or sketching on the go. Water solubility varies, but will usually be indicated on the barrel.

Brush pens—these are available in fiber-tip form or as ones that take an ink cartridge. They provide the versatility of a brush combined with portability and convenience. Some are available double ended, with a brush on one end and a fine marker pen on the other, and are generally specialized in by Japanese manufacturers. Check how waterproof they are before using a wet medium, as they can vary.

Technical (mapping) pen—these provide a constant-thickness ink line and are generally intended for more technical illustration, so are not as versatile at providing an organic-looking ink line. They can, however, be useful for other techniques such as adding stippled texture.

Ballpoint/fountain pen—two surprisingly versatile inking methods. Ballpoint can provide a lovely line, especially for sketching. Being a fixed-width line, it lends itself well to producing tone in a "crosshatch" pattern, i.e. a criss-cross pattern of fixed-width lines. The ink in cheaper ballpoint

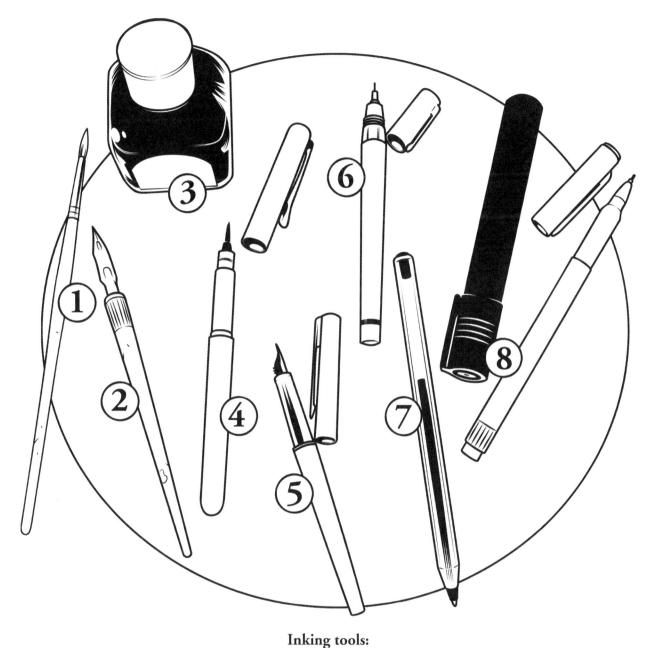

Inking tools:
1. *Brush*   2. *Dip pen with holder and metal nib*   3. *India ink*   4. *Refillable brush pen*
5. *Fountain pen*   6. *Technical (mapping) pen*   7. *Ballpoint pen*   8. *Marker/fiber-tip pens*

pens can go "blobby" after a while and they can be prone to leaking, but are very comfortable to use. The ink can also take a while to dry, so can easily be smudged if you're not careful. A fountain-pen nib is slightly more flexible, but will still give you a fairly fixed line. The advantage of these is that they are refillable and usually have a variety of ink colors available. They don't have to be expensive either—the Platinum Preppy pen, for instance, produces a beautifully smooth line for a fraction of the price of more expensive fountain pens. Ballpoint ink is water-resistant but can spread when wet. Fountain-pen ink is generally water-soluble, however.

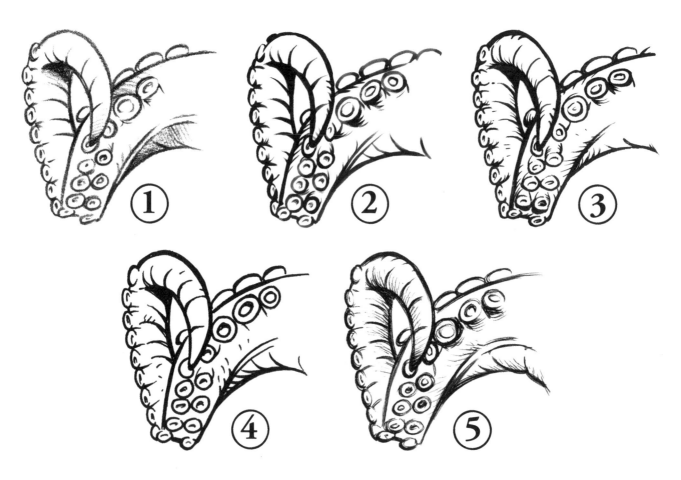

1. *Pencil* 2. *Brush and ink* 3. *Dip pen and ink* 4. *Fiber-tip pen* 5. *Ballpoint pen*

Tone

There are a number of ways of producing tone with ink, other than through the use of linework. All are fairly messy, however! An airbrush can produce a smooth, even tone, but these can be expensive and awkward to use. A more budget alternative is a "blow brush"—generally marketed for children, it's essentially an airbrush through which you blow to spatter paint or ink on to your paper. Even more low-tech is using "toothbrush spatter"—dipping a toothbrush (preferably one you don't clean your teeth with) in ink, then dragging a knife back across it toward you to spatter ink on to the paper. All of these methods will require "masking off" any areas of your artwork on which you don't want the tone (as well as surrounding areas of your workspace). This can be done with torn or cut-up paper or, for a more precise result, with self-adhesive "masking film."

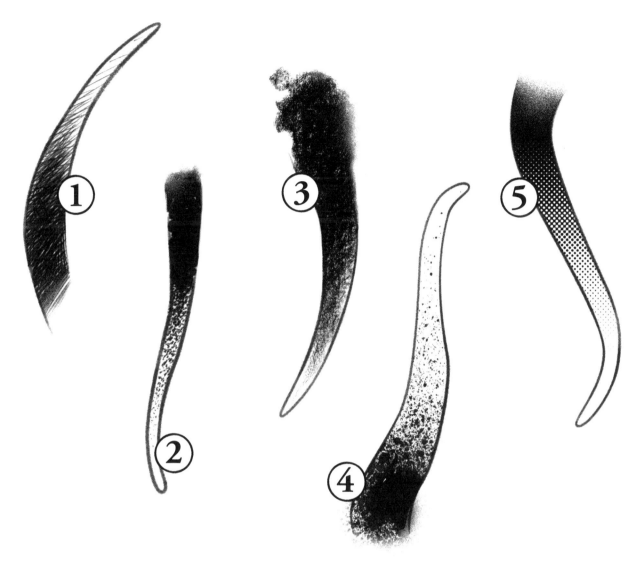

1. *Crosshatch: lines are applied in a number of different directions, getting closer together in areas of denser shadow.*

2. *Stippling: dots of even size are applied, building up their density for darker areas.*

3. *Charcoal or soft pencil: pressure on the paper is increased, depending on the amount of shade required.*

4. *Toothbrush spatter: the closer the toothbrush is to the paper, the greater the density of ink produced. Spatter can also be varied according to how much pressure is applied to the toothbrush when dragging across it.*

5. *Halftone: This is generally applied digitally.*

Which leads us to a less messy alternative, a range of digital options now available…

Digital methods

Digital inking and drawing methods have come a long way in the last few years and there are now many different options available, both on computer and tablet.

Although it is possible to produce linework on a device using a mouse, touchpad, or touch screen, it is far more versatile and creative to use an input method that allows for pressure sensitivity, i.e. a variance in the width of the line according to how hard you press.

Two of the options include:

- Touch screens with pressure-sensitive input, such as the iPad Pro with Apple Pencil or the Wacom Cintiq. These can be very expensive options. Technology is advancing all the time, however, and it's worth searching around for more budget-friendly versions.
- Graphics tablets, such as the Wacom Intuos or Bamboo. The latter particularly is more of a budget option. Be aware, however, that the cheaper tablets are quite small and can lead to repetitive strain injury if used for a long time. A larger tablet is more ergonomic but considerably more expensive.

Whilst input methods for digital art are still quite limited, the range of programs you can use is vast and increasing all the time.

"Vector" programs such as Adobe Illustrator produce a line that is defined by a mathematical formula, rather than by individual pixels. This means that the line can be subsequently repositioned, resized, smoothed out, or replaced with a different

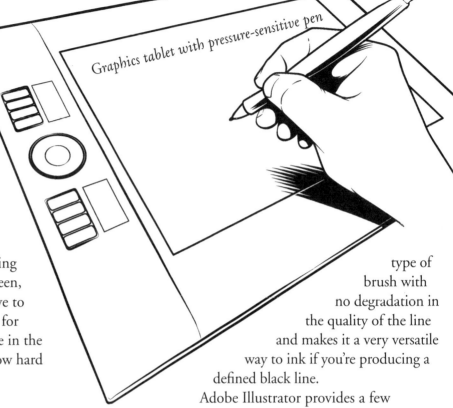

Graphics tablet with pressure-sensitive pen

type of brush with no degradation in the quality of the line and makes it a very versatile way to ink if you're producing a defined black line.

Adobe Illustrator provides a few different brush options, from "calligraphic" brushes, which are pressure-sensitive and act like a hand-drawn dip-pen or brush line, to "art" brushes—defined patterns that spread themselves along the line that you draw, anything from a fixed taper to a rough, chalky texture. Programs like this are becoming more sophisticated all the time and the range of options available is increasing, but these two basic forms of brushes can serve many purposes, especially when combined together.

More painterly programs are also available and can emulate traditional media such as pencil and chalk, whilst providing the versatility of editability and digital manipulation. These are generally pixel-based programs, so be aware of the size at which you are producing the artwork. As with traditional methods of inking, it's always best to work larger than your final image and to reduce the size once you've finished—if your artwork is to be printed, it's always best to work larger than required and to aim for a final output of at least 300 dpi.

Programs such as Clip Studio Paint (formerly Manga Studio) and PaintTool SAI can provide budget or even free alternatives to expensive programs such as Adobe Photoshop. It's worth looking around for what's on offer, especially free software, which you can try out and abandon if you're not getting on with it. These programs also have the advantage of a wide range of coloring and toning capabilities, should you wish to move beyond linework.

Many artists produce rough pencil drawings traditionally and then import these digitally to use as a basis for their final digital inks, although more and more artists are doing the whole process—from rough drawings through to final artwork—entirely digitally.

There are a few other digital techniques that can be very useful for visualizing Lovecraftian creations, such as 3D modelling. Again, there are various free pieces of software available, such as Pixologic's Scupltris, which can be played around with to create all sorts of twisted virtual creations to use as the basis of a drawing. Programs like Adobe Photoshop also have powerful transforming and warping tools that can be used to alter and combine photographic references to fantastic or grotesque effect and can help to kick-start your imagination into life.

And don't forget the power of the image search, a wealth of reference material at your fingertips. Be wary of making your search terms too vague, however, as that's an easy way to get lost in the Internet—think carefully about what it is you're looking for and search accordingly. Searching "wolf," for instance, will give you more results than you can look through in a lifetime, but search for "wolf head in profile" (if that's what you're looking for) and you'll save yourself a lot of time.

Some examples of digital inking:

1. *Adobe Illustrator "calligraphic" brush: pressure sensitive, so that the line thickness varies according to how much pressure is applied.*

2. *Adobe Illustrator "art" brush: a fixed pattern is applied over the length of the brush stroke. The appearance of the pattern will vary according to the length of the stroke.*

3. *Examples of some of the texture and painting brushes available in Clip Studio Paint.*

Note: All the examples in the projects section were inked with Adobe Illustrator, with tone applied in Clip Studio Paint.

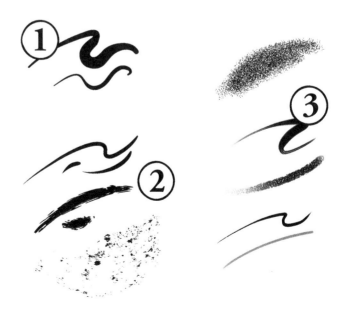

Step-by-step tutorials

GOO/SLIME

1 Start off with a shape made up of a number of overlapping circles to suggest a globular appearance. Add in a few random tendrils snaking off it—keep them quite smooth and fluid to suggest liquidity, but give them several gravity-defying changes in direction to suggest purposefulness. This will contrast with the drips added later.

2 Add in some smaller overlapping globules to the main body. Start to define the tendrils a bit further at some of their changes in direction to suggest their twisting nature. Suggest indentations in the main body at the points where the tendrils are emerging. Add in some small vertically aligned ovals lower down, which will become the ends of some slimy drips. Erase any unnecessary lines.

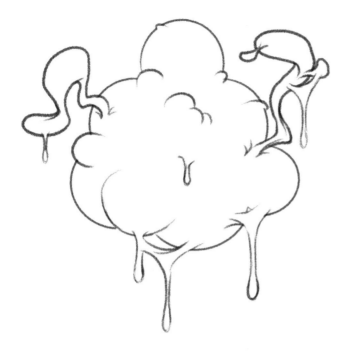

3 Join these up to the main body and tendrils, narrowing these connections with a concave curve toward the drip "heads" as the connecting material stretches. To suggest the non-sentient nature of the drips (as opposed to that of the tendrils), keep the force of gravity acting in the same direction downward on all your drips.

4 Add in some veins on the surface of the main body, some smaller minor tendrils branching off the larger ones and then you're ready to ink up.

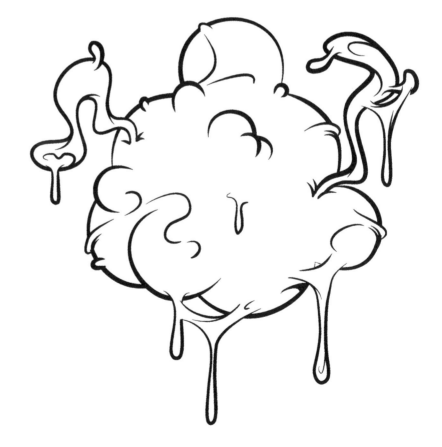

TENTACLES

1 Start off with two curving lines of similar shape, which get closer together toward what will be the tip of the tentacle.

2 Add in a central curving line going roughly diagonally from one edge of the shape to the other. This will define a twisting dividing line between the upper and lower sides of the tentacle. Add a series of paired circles to represent suckers along the length of the tentacle, getting smaller toward the tip and following a similarly curving diagonal line along the length of the tentacle. Add smaller circles within each sucker shape and add some connecting lines behind each to suggest their being joined to the tentacle's body.

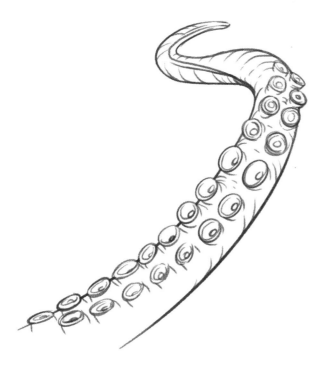

3 Further delineate the suckers' structure by building up their rims. Turn the dividing line between the tentacle's upper and lower sides into a more protruding shape. Add shorter curving lines across the circumference of the tentacle to create a more ridged and rounded appearance.

4 Accentuate the ridges along the edge of the tentacle and add some ridged structure to the flesh connecting each sucker to the tentacle's main body. A strong outline denotes the strength of the beast.

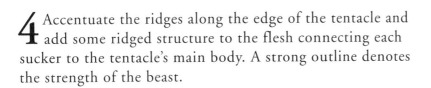

CLAWS

1 Claws come in various shapes and sizes. Take a look at the claws of a sloth compared to that of a prehistoric raptor, for instance. Generally, however, claws will follow a curved shape, ending in a narrow tip. The amount of curvature can vary depending on the type of claw. Draw in your outlines and experiment with the number of claws and their sizes relative to each other—one may be far more prominent than the others, or they may all be of a similar size.

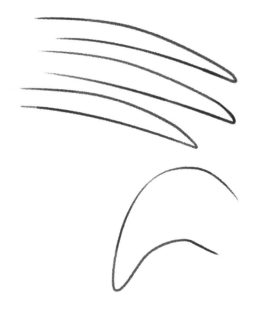

2 Add ridges of various lengths and thicknesses curving along the length of each claw to suggest their bony structure.

3 Add shorter lines across each claw's circumference to suggest its roundness. The way a claw meets a body will vary according to the nature of the creature's flesh: for leathery, scaly, or smooth skin, connect the claws to the body with a ridged appearance.

4 For a more hairy or furred appearance, connect the claws to the body with strokes of varying length and direction, some of these overlapping the join with the claw.

Note: A more twisted initial shape can be used with similar techniques to create any other bony protrusions such as horns, tusks, or teeth.

SPAWN

1 Start off with overlapping circles of similar size. They should get denser and more overlapping toward the edges of the group; less overlapped and more complete toward the center of the group.

2 At the point where some of the circles join each other, flatten the join line to suggest their pressing up against each other. Have a look at the way soap bubbles form or at frogspawn for inspiration.

3 Start to add in some detail—smaller "bubbles" forming off some of the larger ones; some drips; a slimy pool in which the spawn is sitting. Add in a dark, vaguely foetal shape in each of the egg sacs to represent something growing inside.

4 Add in lines to each egg sac to represent a slightly reflective/slimy texture. You could also add in some veins or creatures starting to hatch out. Have a look at the way other spawn, such as toadspawn, looks to give you ideas for other configurations you could come up with.

DECAY

1 This example is going to be a mouth, but these techniques could be applied to any anatomy. Start with a couple of rows of jagged teeth opposite each other and the outline of the outside and inside of the mouth. These teeth are roughly human-looking, so are quite flattened at their ends.

2 Start to add in some flaps of stretched skin and warts or boil-like lumps inside and outside the mouth. Build up some form to the inside and outside of the mouth.

3 Continue to add lumps to the flesh, strands of skin, or saliva stretched across the teeth and skin. Give the flesh a lumpy appearance by overlaying lots of curving shapes—imagine the skin is melting and running down the face like wax on a candle. Cut some small areas out of the figure's outline and join the edges up with jagged tears.

4 Add in some pieces of flesh flaking off and falling away. Continue building up the drippy, lumpy texture, adding in some ridges to the teeth and darkening up the inside of the mouth. Take a look at some zombie makeup effects or, if you're feeling really brave, pictures of skin diseases, for further ideas.

2 **Anemone-like fronds:** overlap longer curving shapes, keeping them roughly triangular, thickening toward their base, with a curved tip on each to suggest softness and fluidity.

OTHER TEXTURES

1 **Scales:** overlap short, curved strokes to suggest overlapping scales. Have a look at fish scales or those of a pangolin or snake for inspiration. Try varying the shape of the scales (more pointed, for instance) to give a different appearance.

3 **Hair/fur:** use a variety of tapered strokes, getting thinner as they move away from the body. Vary the direction, thickness, length, and density of the strokes, getting increasingly denser toward the edge of the body, where they will overlap more.

4 **Spines:** overlap triangular shapes, keeping them straighter and more pointed than those of the anemone fronds, again thickening toward their base where they join onto the main body. Each could also have a slightly convex curve to their sides. Take a look at hedgehog or porcupine spines for inspiration.

5 **Rough hide/skin:** draw similar-sized circles, butting up against each other, interspersed with a few larger ones. Fill in any gaps with smaller circles or ovals. Toward the edge of a figure, start overlapping your shapes in a more similar way to that of scales. Look at alligator or crocodile skin for inspiration.

6 **Bone:** this is similar to drawing claws, but vary the shape to be roughly cylindrical with larger rounded ends for the joints. You could add some extra growths or cut some pieces out of the edge to suggest wear or decay, as well as adding ridges along the bone's length and some small pits on its surface. Take a look at any skeleton—dinosaur bones are particularly dramatic.

PROJECTS

ARWASSA

Arwassa appears in Robert M. Price's short story "Saucers from Yaddith" (1984) and is described as a humanoid torso with tentacles instead of limbs, with a short neck, ending in a toothless, featureless mouth.

I have chosen to give the creature six limbs instead of four to add to its alien appearance and to loosely base its mouth on a fish mouth to add a bit of visual interest, rather than making it entirely featureless.

Visual references: human torso, tentacles, largemouth bass, orange fungus.

STEP 1

Start off with a rough circle for the head, a smaller oval attached to it for the creature's protruding mouth, a larger oval for the torso, and a smaller oval below this for the creature's hips. Roughly bisect the main head shape with two curved lines. The intersection of these will be the position of the creature's eye.

Leave plenty of room around these shapes in order to add in the limbs/tentacles.

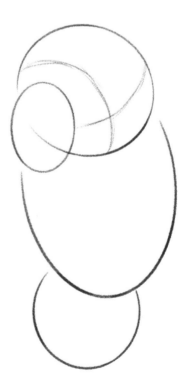

STEP 2

Start to add some detail to the head, sketching in an eye with a heavy fleshy brow above it. Begin to add detail to the mouth area, suggesting upper and lower lip structures. Sketch in ovals on the torso for the beginning positions of the creature's tendrils/tentacles. Start to add in the tentacles behind the creature, keeping them quite wavy and fluid.

STEP 3

Add in tentacles in front of the creature as well, crisscrossing the torso area and each other. Add in two shorter limbs extending from the hip area. Start to add in some ridges and folds to the tentacles, as well as some detail to the head and mouth area—warty lumps, tendrils around the mouth, etc. Darken the area within the mouth and add some structure to the "lips."

STEP 4

Continue to add texture to the tentacles as well as to the torso area, dividing this into chest muscles and the suggestion of a "six-pack" below this. Add in shadow cast by the limbs and body to give the creature more solidity, as well as some slimy strands and drips, and knobbly, warty growths on its limbs. The groin area can be hidden in shadow, but with a gooey, drippy texture suggested.

STEP 5

Add some more musculature to the torso area—the suggestion of ribs and sternum. Continue to build up veins, warts, and drips to give the creature a wet, slimy appearance.

Finally, use tone to accentuate the darkness inside the mouth and the structure of some of the muscles (see the final image).

ATLACH-NACHA

Atlach-Nacha—"The Spider God"—resembles a giant spider with a human-like face. "The face peered up with a weird expression of doubt and inquiry; and terror crawled through the veins of the bold huntsman as he met the small, crafty eyes that were circled about with hair"— "The Seven Geases," Clark Ashton Smith (1934).

This creature is essentially a spider with some humanoid features, but I have chosen to model its body on the structure of a human brain to add to its eeriness. I have also suspended a conglomeration of eggs/spawn below its body to add visual interest.

Visual references: spider, human brain, spawn, spider eggs, human face.

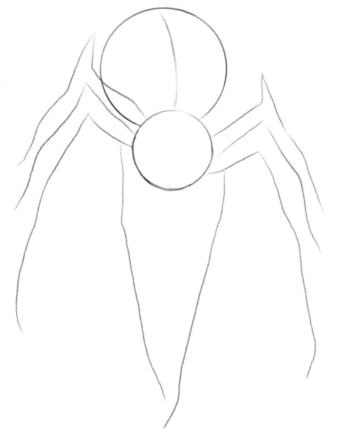

STEP 1

Start with two circles—a larger one for the main body and a smaller one below it for the head. Roughly sketch in four spindly leg shapes on each side, keeping these roughly symmetrical on either side of the body. Bisect the main body with a curved line down the middle, which will divide up the two hemispheres of the creature's "brain."

STEP 2

Add in two human-looking eyes and a small nose toward the base of the creature's head shape, as well as a few more eye shapes around the sides of the head. These can be more arachnid-like—the expression is mostly going to be confined to the central area. Add four ovals to the bottom of the head to represent spider mandibles (its mouthparts). Build up the legs in segments, but still keep them thin and spindly.

STEP 3

Start to build up the facial features—darken the eyes, and add creases around them and around the mandibles. Sketch in some wavy lines over the surface of the "brain." Add hairy texture to the mandibles and stiffer spines to the legs. Roughly sketch in a mass of spawn/eggs behind the creature's legs and hanging below its body.

STEP 4

Start to add detail to the egg sacs (see Spawn on pages 26–27), as well as some slimy drips and web strands between some of the legs.

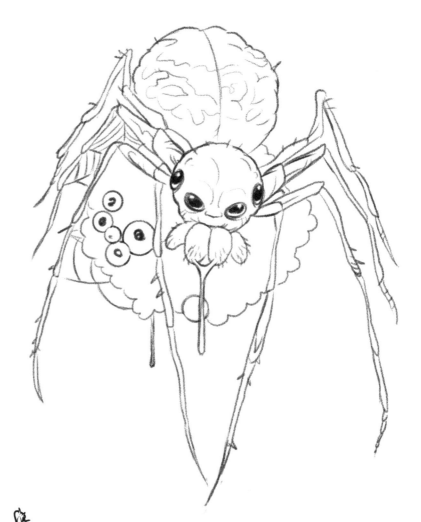

STEP 5

Continue to add in egg-sac shapes with foetal growths. Much of this can be in silhouette, shadowed by the creature's body, as can some of the drips. Add in more webbing and darken up the central divide of the "brain" and some of its ridges. Add a few veins, spiky hairs, etc. to the creature's head for good measure.

Finally, use tone to darken around the edges of the "brain" and around the eyes. Darken the egg sacs underneath the mandibles, leaving these untoned in order to make them stand out better (see the final image).

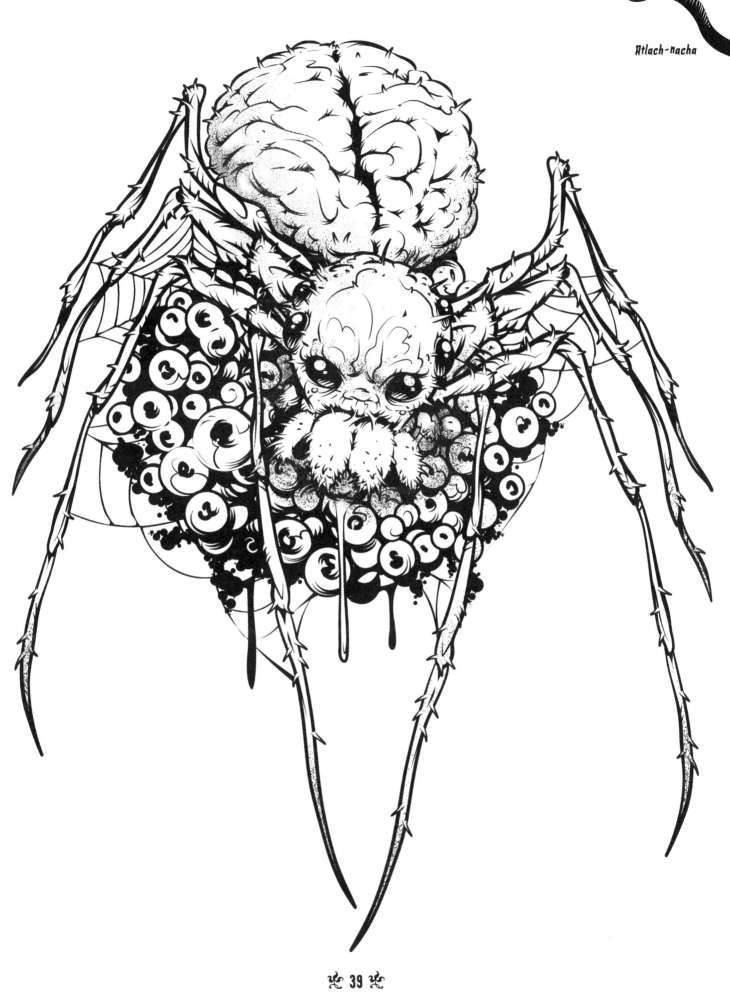

AYLITH

The Aylith is a tall, shadowy female with glowing eyes and protrusions like the branches of a dead tree, first appearing in *Twilight Memoirs* by Clint Krause (2005).

I have chosen to base this design on a Goth-style woman, combined with ancient tree growth.

Visual references: female figure, Goth woman, Victorian corset, dead tree branches.

STEP 1

Start off with a humanoid figure—the body is an "hourglass" shape. The head should be around a quarter of the height of this and is bisected horizontally and vertically into quarters. Each eye will be positioned on the horizontal roughly halfway between each bisection. The bottom of the nose comes roughly two-thirds of the way down the head and the mouth, halfway between the bottom of the nose and the chin.

Use circles at the top of the hourglass shape to represent the points at which the shoulders join and use two roughly equal cylindrical shapes to construct each arm, finished off with a wedge shape to represent the main part of each hand.

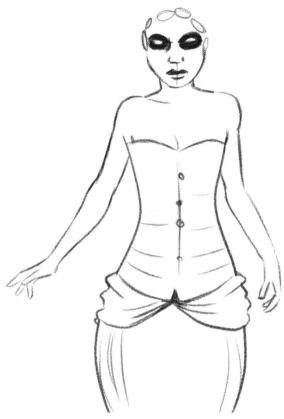

STEP 2

Draw a "crown" of ovals around the circumference of the head shape—these will be the points from which the branches will protrude. Sketch in the outline of a corset shape and add a few folds beneath it to represent some drapes of fabric. Add in some eye shapes and darken around them to accentuate them. Add some detail to the lips and nose and some curvature to the breasts and cleavage. Add in fingers and a thumb to each hand "wedge."

STEP 3

Start to build up the main crisscrossing branches, starting from the ovals around the circumference of the head and gradually getting thinner toward their tips. Vary the direction as you go, keeping the changes in direction jagged and sudden. Add some additional lumps along their lengths to represent knots, galls, and cankers. Draw additional smaller branches coming off these.

STEP 4

Continue to add branches, including below the drapery underneath the corset, from the ends of the fingers, and behind the head and body. Add in some shadows where the branches cross over each other to increase the appearance of depth. Start to add some shading and texture to the corset, suggesting folds going across its width, keeping a highlighted area down the center of each side. Add in some lacy detail around the top of the corset.

Add further detail to the facial features, including some black drips running down the face.

STEP 5

Continue to darken up the corset, adding details such as buttons. Add whorls, knots, etc. to the branches—the more knobbly and twisted they are, the better. Take a look at fungi growing on trees or fallen logs for some ideas, as well as tree growths such as cankers.

Finally, use some tone to further darken the bottom of the corset, underneath the chin, and on some of the branches that are further back, in order to make those in the foreground stand out more (see final image).

BYAKHEE

"They were not altogether crows, nor moles, nor buzzards, nor ants, nor vampire bats, nor decomposed human beings; but something I cannot and must not recall. They flopped limply along, half with their webbed feet and half with their membranous wings."– "The Festival," H. P. Lovecraft (1925).

This is a case of Lovecraft chucking everything into the mix with the hope of creating something weird and unworldly. I have chosen to take elements of each creature, concentrating on an essentially ant-like form.

Visual references: ant, mole, star-nosed mole, bat wings, bird wings, skeletal leg.

STEP 1

Start with a basic ant shape made up of three overlapping circles, a pointed rear, and a circular head tipped with a slight point toward the bottom. Bisect the head shape vertically (the head will end up being segmented into two). Place an oval high up on either side of the head to position the eyes. Sketch two bat-like wings behind the creature's body, roughly symmetrical with each other, but with one wing narrower to suggest it being turned away slightly.

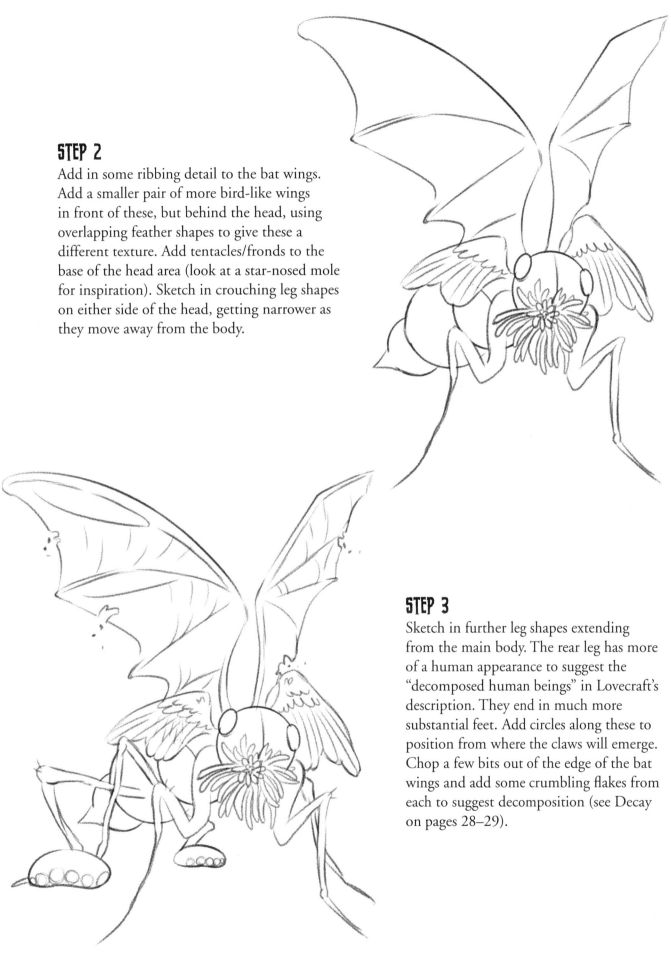

STEP 2

Add in some ribbing detail to the bat wings. Add a smaller pair of more bird-like wings in front of these, but behind the head, using overlapping feather shapes to give these a different texture. Add tentacles/fronds to the base of the head area (look at a star-nosed mole for inspiration). Sketch in crouching leg shapes on either side of the head, getting narrower as they move away from the body.

STEP 3

Sketch in further leg shapes extending from the main body. The rear leg has more of a human appearance to suggest the "decomposed human beings" in Lovecraft's description. They end in much more substantial feet. Add circles along these to position from where the claws will emerge. Chop a few bits out of the edge of the bat wings and add some crumbling flakes from each to suggest decomposition (see Decay on pages 28–29).

STEP 4

Add curving, roughly equal-sized claws coming from the rear feet. Add a smaller "thumb" claw around the side (look at mole feet for inspiration). Darken up the main body. Add bristly hairs to the legs and elsewhere, as well as some strands of stretched skin to the rear legs. Firm up the dividing ridge along the head.

STEP 5

Build up the ridges around each eye and the texture of the bird and bat wings. Add ridges along the length of the claws and the insect legs, as well as further warty texture on these and on the creature's head.

Finally, use tone to darken the tips of the bat wings, the main body, around the eyes, and behind the "mouth tentacles" to make these stand out (see the final image).

47

CHTHONIAN

"**F**lowing tentacles and pulpy grey-black, elongated sack of a body... no distinguishing features at all other than the reaching, groping tentacles. Or was there—yes—a lump in the upper body of the thing... a container of sorts for the brain, basal ganglia, or whichever diseased organ governed this horror's loathsome life!"— *The Burrowers Beneath,* Brian Lumley (1974).

Visual references: tapeworm, sea worm, squid tentacles, lamprey mouth, sun starfish.

STEP 1

Start with several thick, overlapping curved segments. These will form the creature's twisted, worm-like body. Draw a circular shape for the head, with a smaller circle inside it—this will become the creature's mouth.

STEP 2

Radiating out from the mouth area, draw ten or so roughly equally spaced short tentacles of a similar size. Contrast these with several longer, more flowing tentacles, branching back from the same area along the length of the body. Position these in front of the head shape but behind the shorter radiating tentacles. Add in a circle of inward-pointing teeth to the edge of the mouth.

STEP 3

Connect up the body sections and add ridges along their length and across their circumference. Start to add in some veins along the body sections and ridges down the center of each of the shorter tentacles. Add a lumpy, ganglia-like mass on top of the head, behind the tentacles. Add in further rows of teeth to the mouth.

STEP 4

Add in suckers along the length of each long tentacle and smaller protuberances along each shorter tentacle (look at starfish tentacles for inspiration). Build up the lumpiness of the ganglia and add shadows cast by the tentacles and inside the mouth.

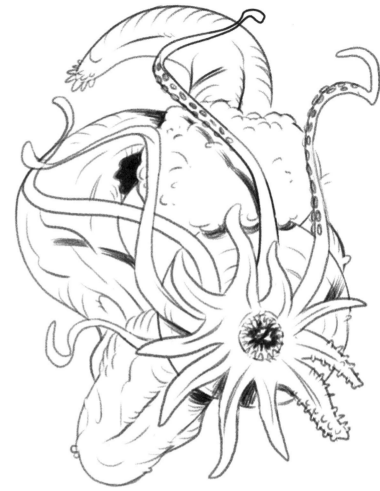

STEP 5

Continue to add protuberances, suckers, etc. Build up the depth of some of the ridges on the body and around the head.

Use tone to accentuate the roundness of the body, the lumpiness of the ganglia, and to darken behind the tentacles (see the final image).

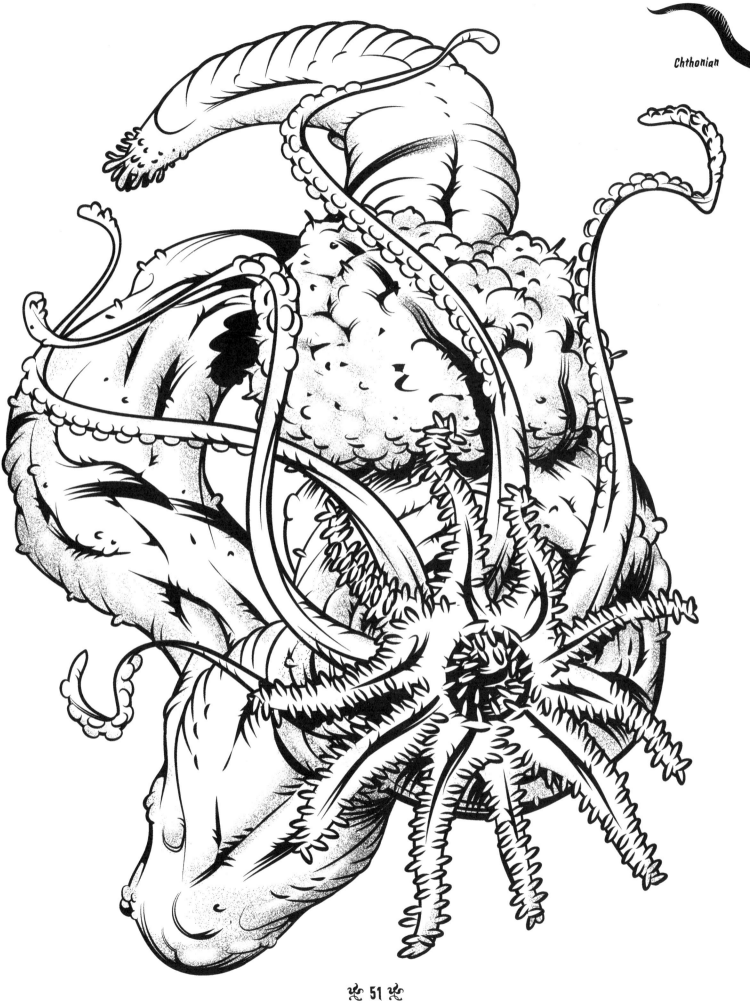

Chthonian

CTHULHU

Cthulhu is described in H. P. Lovecraft's story "The Call of Cthulhu" (1928) as "a monster of vaguely anthropoid outline, but with an octopus-like head whose face was a mass of feelers, a scaly, rubbery-looking body, prodigious claws on hind and fore feet, and long, narrow wings behind."

I have chosen to give my version of Cthulhu a bulkier form than Lovecraft's original sketch, drawing on an ape-like body structure in addition to the cephalopod-like features of the creature's head.

Visual references: octopus, squid, gorilla, raptor claws, bat/gargoyle wings.

STEP 1

Start with a curving outline, curling around into branching, swirling lines, which are going to become the creature's squid-like face. It is not going to have any discernible neck, so the line of its back flows into the bulge of the head and its vestigial tail in one smooth curve. Position the eye somewhere up near the apex of this curve, above the leftmost tentacle line.

STEP 2

Build up the bulk of the tentacles, keeping them smooth and fluid (see Tentacles on pages 22–23). Add in some ragged-looking, folded bat-like wings sprouting from its back. These are fairly vestigial-looking, rather than being designed for flight. Add a lumpy brow above the eye and some boil-like growths on the creature's head and tentacles, as well as making the outline of the back more lumpy.

STEP 3

Continue to add details around the eye and on to the wings. Start to add rows of suckers along the tentacles—bear in mind that many of the suckers will be concealed by the bulk of some of the tentacles. Starting with the shoulder slightly below and left of the creature's eye, sketch in a straightened ape-like arm shape—look at the stance of a gorilla and the shape of its forearm for inspiration. The rear leg is more dinosaur/horse-like in contrast, so it bends backward and then forward again.

STEP 4

Add an octopoid pupil (rectangular) in the center of the eyeball. Start to add in some skin markings on the back and shoulder and claws on the end of the rear feet. The larger curved claw is inspired by those of a prehistoric velociraptor. There is also a further "spur" claw positioned on the back joint of the leg. A second leg can be sketched in behind the creature's body, as well as a second arm. Both of these can mostly be in silhouette in the shadow cast by the creature's body.

STEP 5

You can now add in some drips of moisture or slime, veins over the skin's surface, and some warty growths to give the skin more texture. Further shadows cast by the creature's tentacles will serve to give a feeling of bulk to your creation.

Use tone to darken around the eye, to delineate the wings from each other, and to shape the creature's muscles and swollen growths (see the final image).

DZEWA

D zewa, or "The White God" is a plant god created by the writer Ramsey Campbell in the short story "The Insects from Shaggai" (1964). It is described on The H. P. Lovecraft Wiki as: "a great white orb hiding an enormous magenta excrescence, like an orchid or lamprey mouth with emerald tentacles emerging from the mass."

I have tried to suggest a plant-like base to the creature, while incorporating some signs of bestial intelligence and a ravenous appetite.

Visual references: lamprey mouth, starfish tentacles, tropical leaves, tree tumor, tree canker, fish eyes, Orchidaceae.

STEP 1

Start off with five leaf shapes radiating out from a central circle, which will become the creature's mouth. Keep the leaf edges fairly fluid and wobbly, ending in a pointed tip. We will adjust each leaf's outline as we go along. Draw a line indicating a central vein along the middle of each leaf shape.

STEP 2

Radiating from the same central circle, add in some tentacle shapes (see Tentacles on pages 22–23). Don't add suckers to these, as they're going to have more of a starfish appearance. From the central circle, add a tendril of a more uniform thickness, leading to a circle roughly below that of the mouth area, which is going to become the creature's tumorous "excrescence."

STEP 3

Start to add some details—several radiating, overlapping sets of pointed teeth in the central circle (look at a lamprey mouth for inspiration), minor veins radiating out from each of the leaves' central veins, and fish-like eyes in between the tentacles. On the lower circle, add overlapping curves that get denser toward the edge of the circle, to create a lumpy, spherical-looking surface. Start adding some veins to the excrescence's "stalk." Erase parts of some of the leaf edges and add in more jagged lines to suggest bite marks or decay in the leaf edges. Thicken up each central leaf vein slightly.

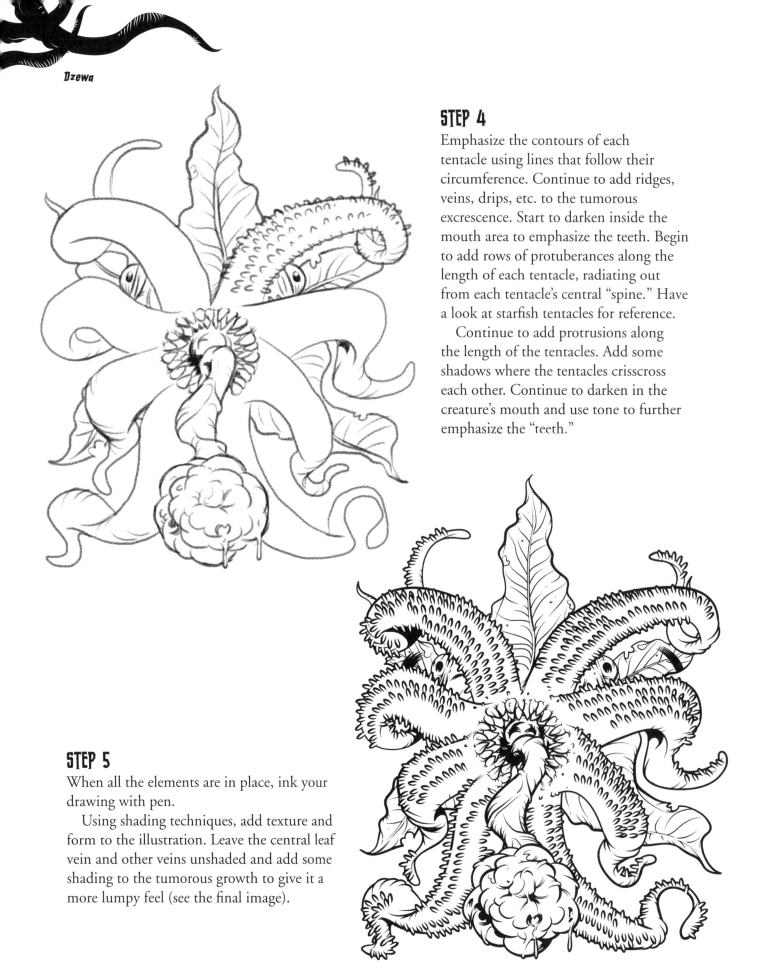

Dzewa

STEP 4

Emphasize the contours of each tentacle using lines that follow their circumference. Continue to add ridges, veins, drips, etc. to the tumorous excrescence. Start to darken inside the mouth area to emphasize the teeth. Begin to add rows of protuberances along the length of each tentacle, radiating out from each tentacle's central "spine." Have a look at starfish tentacles for reference.

Continue to add protrusions along the length of the tentacles. Add some shadows where the tentacles crisscross each other. Continue to darken in the creature's mouth and use tone to further emphasize the "teeth."

STEP 5

When all the elements are in place, ink your drawing with pen.

Using shading techniques, add texture and form to the illustration. Leave the central leaf vein and other veins unshaded and add some shading to the tumorous growth to give it a more lumpy feel (see the final image).

FORMLESS SPAWN

"**F**ar worse—they were amorphous lumps of viscous black slime that took temporary shapes for various purposes."—H. P. Lovecraft & Zealia Bishop, "The Mound" (first published 1940).

Taking my cue from the name, I have chosen to depict this creature as fairly random clumps of spawn joined by liquid-looking interlinking flesh.

Visual references: spawn, soft coral.

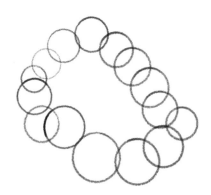

STEP 1

Start with several circular areas marked out to contain your clumps of spawn. Begin to add in smaller circles within each of these, to represent the spawn eggs.

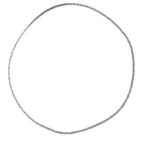

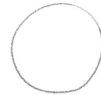

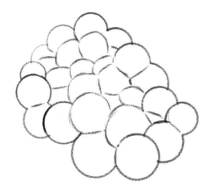

STEP 2

Join some of these eggs together with straighter lines to suggest their pressing up against each other (see Spawn on pages 26–27). Continue to do this for all the clumps of spawn, adding a few smaller clumps and isolated eggs dotted around and between the larger clumps.

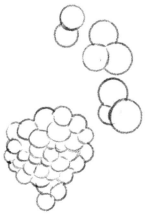

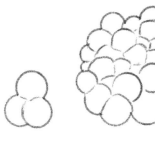

STEP 3

Start to join up the clumps with flowing, amorphous lines. This is "formless spawn," so there's really no right or wrong way to do this, but give your lines a bit of twist and dynamism, if possible. Add a few smaller shapes branching off the main "trunks" and a few even smaller growths branching off those, as if the creature's flesh is constantly fractally moving and reforming itself.

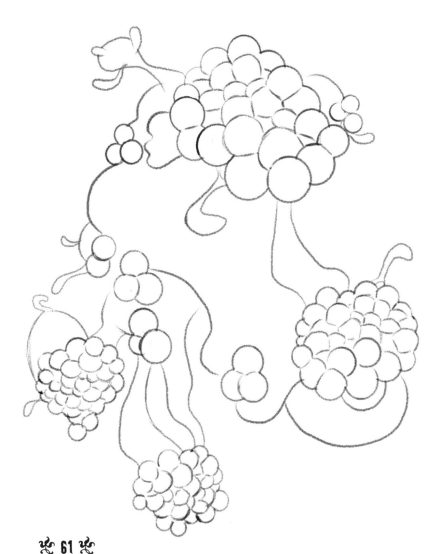

STEP 4

Add some twisting texture to the main trunks, partially formed eggs, and growths growing out of the flesh, veins, etc. At the ends of some of the smaller growths, add spawn eggs starting to form, almost resembling eyeballs. Add some dripping goo (see Goo/slime on pages 20–21) and dark foetal shapes in the center of most of the eggs.

STEP 5

Intensify some of the shading in the trunks' creases and add shadows cast by the clumps of spawn, criss-crossing trunks, and tendrils, etc. to give the creature some defined form (even though it's described as "formless").

Use tone around the edges of the eggs and along the edges of the trunks to suggest their cylindrical shape (see the final image).

GHOUL

"The bodies, while roughly bipedal, had a forward slumping, and a vaguely canine cast. The texture of the majority was a kind of unpleasant rubberiness." First described in H. P. Lovecraft's story "Pickman's Model" (1927), the Ghoul has similar attributes to that of a classic werewolf figure.

I have chosen to contrast a smooth-skinned humanoid body with furrier textures and a number of canine features.

Visual references: snarling dog, wolf, canine spine, crouching man.

STEP 1

Begin with a torso shape with a circle for the hips close to the ground, to suggest the figure is going to be in a squatting position, making it look bestial. Form an oval where the shoulder joins the torso, then construct the creature's forearm using two roughly equal-sized ovals and a wedge shape for its hand/front paw. This paw will be resting on the ground in the final drawing, which should give you a guide as to the positioning of the hips.

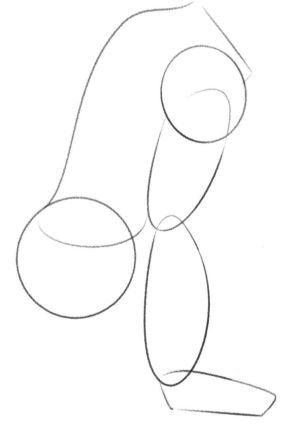

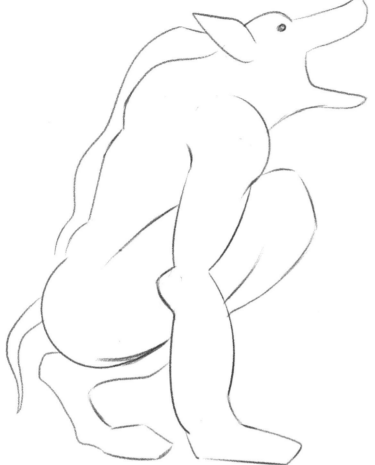

STEP 2

Join up the arm shapes, adding a protruding elbow. From the neck, sketch in a dog head shape—long curved jaws with a good wide opening between them, a small eye near the top of the head with a prominent brow above it, and a backward-pointing ear behind the eye. Add in a guideline following the line of the back at a little distance from it—this will form the extent of the creature's bony spine. Carry that curve on below the bottom of the back into a stubby tail shape. Draw a dog leg shape below the hips—pointing backward then forward again to end in a wedge-shaped paw. Join this to the body with the creature's knee protruding in line with the middle of its lower jaw.

STEP 3

Draw a series of bony protuberances emerging from the creature's back, using the guideline you've already drawn to give them a flowing curve. These bones should emerge perpendicularly from the back, so the angle should vary according to their position. Look at a human or canine spine for inspiration. Segment the tail section into separate bones. Add rows of pointed teeth along each jaw, a tongue shape, and detail around the eye and snout. Start to build up the musculature on the torso and legs and add some hairy texture to the head and ends of the leg and arm. Add some pointed claws to both paw shapes.

STEP 4

Continue to build up the muscles, fur, veins, etc., adding some drips and strands of drool and saliva. Keep the main body quite smooth, using longer, flowing lines to contrast with the more broken-up lines of the furred forearm, paws, and snout.

STEP 5

Darken under the lower jaw and around the mouth, as well as adding shadows cast by the creature's body under its armpit, below its hips, on its tail, etc. The creature's second leg and arm are mostly obscured and can be added in largely using silhouette.

Use tone to emphasize the darker areas under the hips and lower and upper jaws, etc. (see the final image).

GLAAKI

The Glaaki first appeared in Ramsey Campbell's story "The Inhabitant of the Lake" (1964). Its appearance is that of an enormous slug covered with metallic spines and extruding tentacles.

Being a water dweller, I have given the Glaaki a gravity-defying structure inspired by sea slugs and sea anemones, incorporating two distinct upper and lower forms to its extruded growths.

Visual references: sea slug, sea anemone, sea cucumber, slug, bracket fungus and rose or bramble thorns.

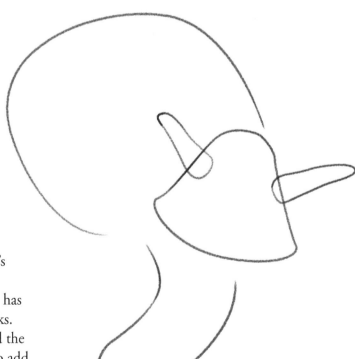

STEP 1

Begin with a bell shape for the creature's head with short, rounded cone shapes extending from either side. Although it has no eyes as such, these will be its eyestalks. Draw a hunched S-shaped body behind the head, leaving plenty of room above it to add in its upper protrusions.

STEP 2

Start to add in a series of long overlapping, flowing, and curving anemone-like fronds along the length of the creature's upper "spine." Contrast these with shorter, spikier cone-shaped growths emerging from the lower half of the creature's body. Look at sea cucumbers or bramble or rose thorns for inspiration. Fringe the bottom half of the creature's head with a couple of overlapping wavy rows similar to that of some bracket fungi. Where the creature's eyetalks join its head, build up some ridges around the bases of the stalks.

STEP 3

Continue to add in upper and lower protrusions, keeping the upper ones smooth and the lower ones spiky. Delineate a ridge denoting the upper and lower sections of the body and add some darker markings to the bell-shaped head to create more of a focus in that area.

Glaaki

STEP 4

Add in some extra random tentacles behind the creature's body with smaller extrusions emerging from the ends of these. Also add a slimy drip or two, especially coming from the mouth. Darken under the head and body where they are casting shade, as well as under some of the spikes. Give each of the longer upper-body growths a dark central core.

STEP 5

Continue to do this for all of the upper fronds. Add in some smaller, warty protuberances and vestigial tentacles/spikes, etc.

Use tone to darken behind and under the head area to give it more emphasis. Darken the more shaded areas around the base of the upper fronds to make them stand out (see the final image) and add anything else you feel would enhance your illustration.

Glaaki

KTHAW'KETH

Kthaw'keth is a more recent addition to the Cthulhu Mythos, appearing in Lovecraftian comic book fan-fiction. It is also known as "The Supreme Unknown, Scourge of Yaksh" and has been described as a six-eyed, crocodile-snouted monstrosity with both tentacles and tripod-like limbs.

I have chosen to emphasize the triple nature of the creature by incorporating three tails, three legs, and three toes. In line with its crocodilian nature, I have given it a fairly dinosaur-like, solid appearance.

Visual references: crocodile, alligator, elephant, giant tube worms, Dimetrodon.

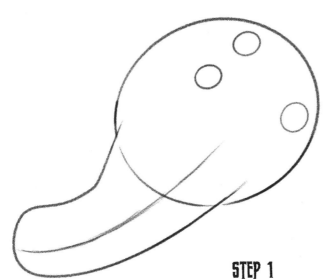

STEP 1

Begin with an oval for the main part of the head with a curved duck-bill-like snout extending from it. Roughly mark in ovals for three of the creature's eyes (assuming the head is symmetrical, three of its six eyes will be obscured by its head). Bisect the "bill" shape with an upward-curving line, which will be a guide for the creature's rows of teeth.

STEP 2

Darken around the eyes and build up a ridge shape above each one. Also add ridges toward the end of the snout, which will surround the creature's nostrils. Draw in an upper curve for the line of the creature's back behind the head and a more triangular line above this to create a fin along the backbone. Extend three stout, cylindrical legs from the main body, dividing each into three solid toes at their ends.

STEP 3

Add in some detail to the head—rows of triangular teeth, some pointing upward from the lower jaw, some pointing downward from the upper jaw to interlock with each other. Look at a crocodile's jawline for inspiration. Add a narrow pupil to each of the eyes. Draw ridges along the fin and around each leg—look at the texture of an elephant's leg for inspiration. Add stubby claws/toenails to the end of each toe and add in three stubby tails behind the main body.

Kthaw'keth

STEP 4

Build up the rough texture of the creature's skin (see Other Textures on page 30), adding some saliva drool around the mouth if you haven't already done so. Add shadows cast by the head onto the upper and lower body, the legs, and the tails, which will help to give your creature a feeling of bulk and solidity. Add a crest of intertwining tentacles at the back of the head, with one or two flopping over the top of the head. The shape of these is inspired by giant tube worms.

STEP 5

Continue to build up the rough texture of the skin and detail in the tentacle crest and claws/toenails.

Use tone to emphasize the roughness of the skin, leaving the more prominent raised areas white. Darken around the eyes and at the bottom of the fin (see the final image).

NIGHTGAUNT

The Nightgaunt appears in H. P. Lovecraft's story *The Dream-quest of Unknown Kadath* (first published in 1943). It is described as being vaguely human, but thin, black, and faceless, with slick rubbery skin, inward-facing horns, a long barbed tail, and prehensile paws.

Rather than making the creature entirely faceless, I have chosen to base its features on that of an eyeless whale, with some other animal features incorporated into the mix. It has a vaguely hunched humanoid appearance to suggest some malevolent intelligence.

Visual references: blue whale, ram horns, scorpion tail, otter paws, bat/gargoyle wings.

STEP 1

Begin with an oval for the creature's head. It's not going to have a body as such—limbs, tail, wings, etc. will all come off this main shape. Bisect it with a curved line about two-thirds of the way down to form its mouth. Sketch in arm shapes using two thin cylinders for each and a wedge shape for the hand. Try to suggest a hunched/crouching attitude with the positioning of the arms.

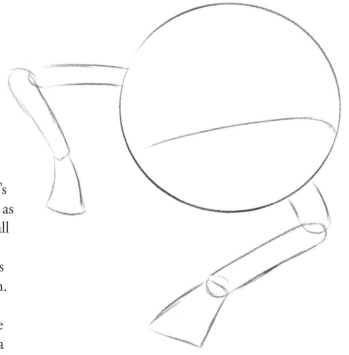

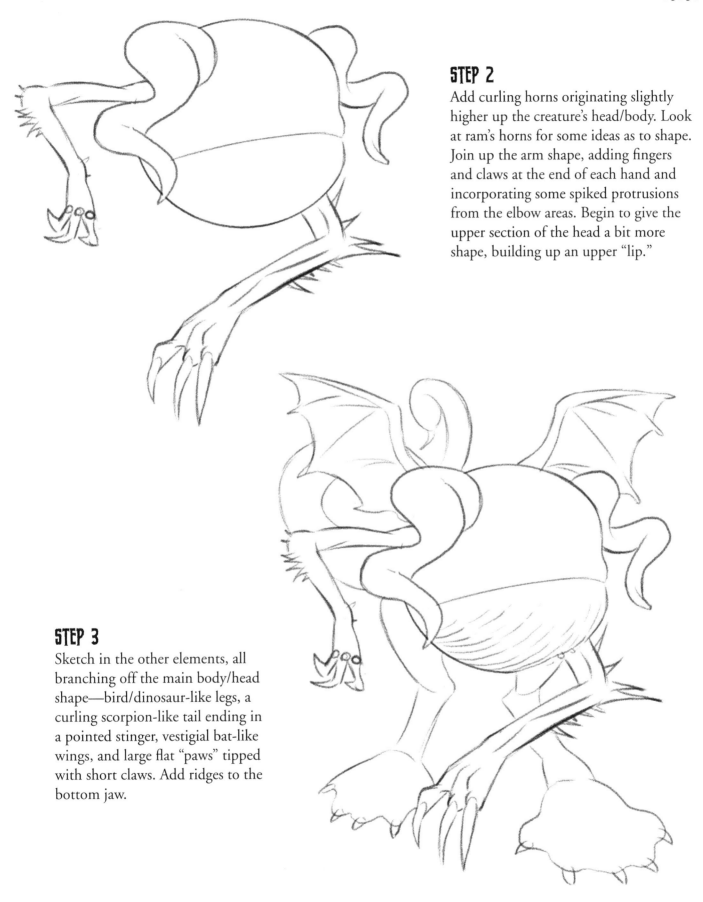

STEP 2

Add curling horns originating slightly higher up the creature's head/body. Look at ram's horns for some ideas as to shape. Join up the arm shape, adding fingers and claws at the end of each hand and incorporating some spiked protrusions from the elbow areas. Begin to give the upper section of the head a bit more shape, building up an upper "lip."

STEP 3

Sketch in the other elements, all branching off the main body/head shape—bird/dinosaur-like legs, a curling scorpion-like tail ending in a pointed stinger, vestigial bat-like wings, and large flat "paws" tipped with short claws. Add ridges to the bottom jaw.

STEP 4

Add different textures to the various parts of the creature—fur around the paws, overlapping plates along the tail, bony ridges along the length of the horns, etc. Darken up the upper part of the head, suggesting a smooth slickness and add shadows cast by the head on its legs and arms. In the silhouetted area around what would be the creature's groin, suggest some dripping putrescence and add some broken-up furry blackness to the top of the creature's paws.

STEP 5

Continue to add texture to the horns, wings, arms, etc., incorporating some foamy drool emerging from the creature's mouth if you haven't already done so.

Use tone to darken under the tail, at the base of the wings, and to further darken the upper part of the creature's head, leaving a highlighted area around the edge to suggest a smooth reflectiveness (see the final image).

NYCTELIOS

Nyctelios is described in "Le Regard Dans l'Abime" by Patrick Bosquet as an exiled deity, manifesting on his return as a blue, six-meter tall, cyclops-like monstrosity, with the bulk of his body covered entirely in crawling worms.

This is essentially a human figure with a cyclopean eye, but I have used a bodybuilder's extreme physique as a basis, imagining the protruding veins on their body turning into the worms in which Nyctelios is covered.

Image references: bodybuilder, cyclops, worms.

STEP 1

Start with the basics of a crouching human figure. Begin with an oval for the head bisected vertically and horizontally. Keep the horizontal bisection slightly lower than halfway down the head and slightly curve it to suggest that the face is pointing downward a little. The creature's single eye will be placed at the intersection of the two bisecting lines. Build up the foreground arm using a circle for the shoulder, two similar-sized ovals, and a wedge shape for the hand. Keep the ovals quite stout and wide, as the physique is going to be stocky and well-muscled. Use similar, smaller shapes to construct a second arm behind and pointing away from the head.

STEP 2

Connect up the arm shapes and add fingers to each hand. The ones in front could be splayed out, as if pressed against the ground. Add a single, oversized eye at the intersection of the two bisecting lines on the head and an open mouth shape toward the bottom of the oval. Build up the shape of the torso behind the head and front arm. As the figure is in a crouching position, much of the hips and top of the legs will be obscured by its posture, but construct the legs in a similar way to the arms, using two ovals for each and a triangular wedge for the foot that is visible.

STEP 3

Start adding some muscular structure to the arms and legs. Take a look at the overly developed musculature of a male bodybuilder to get some ideas, but basically add lumpy ovals to the surface of the body to represent bulging muscles. Start to add veins over the surface and worm shapes emerging from the creature's flesh, particularly clustered around the mouth area. Place the hip area under the torso in shadow.

STEP 4

Continue to add worms. Have some of them fully emerged from the body, some of them in the process of emerging, and some still vein-like protrusions on the skin's surface. Do this by using shadows cast by the worms to suggest distance from the flesh and by erasing linework where the worms are in contact with the skin.

STEP 5

Continue to add worms and give some of them detail by drawing ridges around their circumference. Take a look at an earthworm to see their ridged, segmented appearance. Some worms that are in shadow can be represented purely in silhouette. Add some toe details to the visible foot and fingernails to the hands, and strengthen up the lines of the musculature.

Finally, use some tone to further define the muscles and darken around the eye and mouth (see the final image).

Star Vampire

First appearing in Robert Bloch's story "The Shambler From The Stars" (1935), a Star Vampire is described as: "Red and dripping; an immensity of pulsing, moving jelly; a scarlet blob with myriad tentacular trunks that waved and waved. There were suckers on the tips of the appendages, and these were opening and closing with a ghoulish lust."

This creature is a space dweller, so has a gravity-defying appearance. I have tried to suggest its leech-like nature using sea cucumbers and sea anemones as inspiration with lamprey-like mouths.

Visual references: sea cucumber, sea anemone, lamprey mouth.

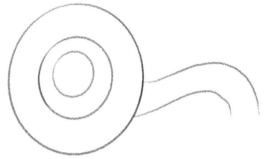

STEP 1

Start with two similarly sized sets of three ovals. These will be guidelines for the creatures "heads," their tentacles, teeth, and mouth parts. Add in a "stalk" from each of the heads—these will end up winding around each other in a congealed central mass.

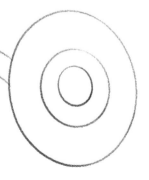

STEP 2

On each head, draw a series of overlapping, wavy tentacles radiating out from the center, each starting roughly from the guideline of the middle oval in each "head." Within this middle oval, draw shorter outward-pointing protrusions radiating around the center. Continue to do this in smaller and smaller circles, ending with a circle of inward-pointing "teeth," which will form the creature's mouth. Repeat this for the other "head." Add in a central vein along each "stalk," as well as frilled edges and ridges across the circumference of each.

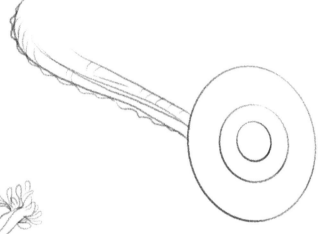

STEP 3

Continue to add "stalks," crisscrossing and entwining with each other. End any free-floating stalks in groups of anemone-like tentacles, similar to those on the heads. Darken within the mouth areas of each head, accentuating the teeth. Add some saliva/mucus strands strung across each mouth.

STEP 4

Build up the "stalks" further, adding some shadows where overlapping stalks would cast them, to give the structure some three-dimensionality.

STEP 5

Continue to add texture to the creature's "body"—small protrusions emerging along the stalks' length, a ridged structure, and central ridged veins.

Use tone to accentuate the cylindrical shape of the body stalks and darken around the mouth areas, leaving the teeth white in order to accentuate them (see the final image).

TSATHOGGUA

Created by Clark Ashton Smith in his story "The Tale of Satampra Zeiros" (first published 1931), Tsathoggua is described as "very squat and pot-bellied. His head was more like a monstrous toad than a deity, and his whole body was covered with an imitation of short fur, giving somehow a vague sensation of both the bat and the sloth. His sleepy lids were half-lowered over his globular eyes; and the tip of a queer tongue issued from his fat mouth."

I have gone for a monstrous toad-like appearance in my depiction, with elements of bat and sloth mixed in.

Visual references: cane toad, bat/gargoyle wings, sloth.

STEP 1

Begin with two ovals: one for the head, and a larger one behind it for the body. Add two triangles sticking up at the top of the head, which will become the ridged protrusions above the creature's eyes. Bisect the head oval with a downward-curved line about a third of the way down, which will become the mouth.

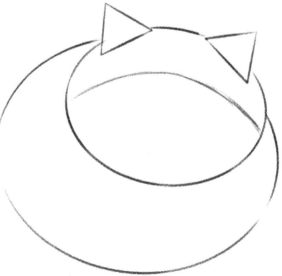

STEP 2

Add some detail to the head—a lumpy texture around the bottom of the head, suggesting pustular growths; small, beady eyes below the brows; and a lumpier texture for the line of the mouth. Add in the creature's human-like arms using circles for the shoulders and two ovals for the upper and lower parts of each arm. Make the forearm ovals somewhat larger than those of the upper arm. Add in roughly symmetrical bat-wing shapes behind the head. Take a look at classic gargoyle statues for inspiration for the wing shape.

STEP 3

Add veins and ribbing to the wings. Continue to add warty pustules to the lower half of the head and build up the ridge of the upper "lip." Build up creases/ridges around the eyes and darken the eyes themselves, leaving a white highlight in each. Add veins to the upper arms, some small rough warts to the shoulders, and a hairier/furrier texture to the forearms. Tip each forearm with three similar-sized, gently curving claws, along the lines of a sloth's.

STEP 4

Add plenty of drool from the creature's mouth, shadow beneath the lower part of its head, and the suggestion of hind toad-like legs, which will mostly be obscured by the creature's squatting posture.

STEP 5

Continue to add texture to the skin and wings, concentrating particularly on the head and around the eyes. Make the fur texture denser underneath the forearms to suggest it's in shade.

Accentuate this with tone as well as darkening the bottoms of the wings, underneath the rear legs, and defining the muscles of the chest area and upper arms (see the final image).

VTHYARILOPS

Vthyarilops, the "Starfish God" is "a tentacled horror similar to a Sun Star, but endowed with branching tentacles, spines, myriads of blue glaring eyes, and gaping-maws"–The H. P. Lovecraft Wiki.

For my version of Vthyarilops, I have chosen to combine several different types of tentacles, drawing on octopus, squid, and starfish.

Visual influences: squid, octopus, starfish, compound eyes, sea urchin.

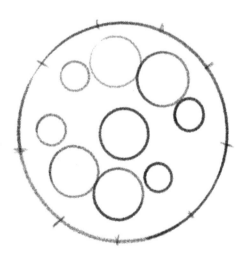

STEP 1

Start with a small circle, leaving plenty of room around it to allow for branching tentacles. Divide the circumference into nine or ten equal divisions as a guide for attaching the tentacles. Draw a series of smaller circles within the main one, which will become the creature's multiple eyes.

STEP 2

Begin to add tentacles to the central structure. Start with two squid-like tentacles of nearly constant width and end them in flatter, splayed ends. Begin to add small circles within the eye shapes to create compound, insect-like eyes.

STEP 3

Using the divisions around the edge of the central circle as a guide, start to add two more forms of tentacles to the "head"—longer, flowing octopus-like tentacles and shorter starfish-like tentacles. Start to add some more details to the squid-like tentacles from step 2—frilled edges along their tips, ridges along their length, and veins.

STEP 4

Continue to add detail to the compound eyes, introduce paired rows of suckers to the longer tentacles, and elongated mouth-like openings to some of the shorter tentacles. Each of these could also have a smaller tentacle/tongue reaching out of it. Behind the main body, add in radiating and overlapping spiky structures, similar to those of a sea urchin's spines.

STEP 5

Continue to build up the texture of the suckers, eyes, mouths, etc., adding some mucus-like strands and drips of saliva to the mouth/tongue structures and smaller protuberances along the lengths of the starfish-like tentacles. Use some shadow to darken within the mouths and underneath the body.

Finally, add some tone to the rear sea-urchin-like spikes to accentuate the main body, as well as along the edges of the tentacles to give them a more cylindrical appearance (see the final image).

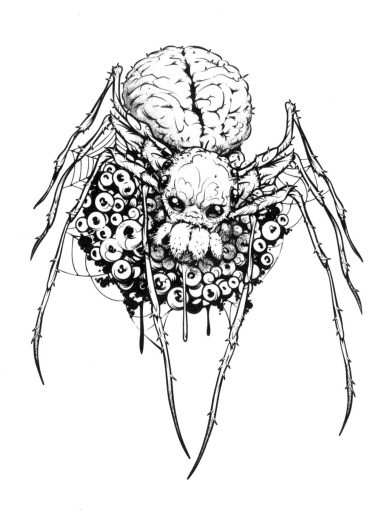